A Stranger Passing Through

I0087368

By A.G. Allums

Published in Easton, Pennsylvania by Allums Publishing.

Allums Publishing Titlles may be purchased in bulk for educational, business, fund-raising, or sales promotional use. For information, please email allumspublishing@outlook.com.

ISBN 978-0-578-62875-2

Table Of Contents

Preface

For You

For Me

For God

Mapacha: A Short Story

Preface

I once read a Facebook post that said, "to be absent from the drama, is to be present with the peace" and the following is a collection of poetry and prose that was created during my transition from "drama" to "peace".

In the fall semester of my junior year of high school, my mother passed away. While much of my childhood I don't remember, I do remember this: she was not a good mother. When she passed away, I shed only a few tears for the crowd of people around me so as not to be deemed heartless by my community. Needless to say, my life improved significantly after her passing. I have since grown to pity her and although she is no longer here, I have forgiven her for not being the mother I needed her to be. Only by understanding that she grew up in a family where her trauma could not be addressed in the ways that ours today can be addressed, was I able to forgive. For that reason, I no longer wish ill will to her legacy and I hope that she is resting in peace.

After my mother's passing, I moved away from my crazy, drug infested childhood home and began fending for myself along with the help of an amazing tribe of mentors, father figures, church family and teachers.

The next year, on my 18th birthday, I lost my grandmother… And *that's* when all hell broke loose. My grandmother essentially raised me, and her love and prayers are the only reason I'm alive and well today. I fell into the pits of depression but managed to somehow finish high school as a full international baccalaureate student with honors. I later went on to attain a bachelor's degree in business finance from Kansas State University. Academic achievement had always been her ode to preach over myself and my three younger brothers; so at each milestone, I honored her for her investment of prayer and uplift because I know that she is somewhere watching me… and I know that she is proud.

My grandmother was a minister and missionary in the COGIC church for about 40 years of her life and I watched her trust God for everything… every day. Much of my writing includes allusions and metaphors that relate to my COGIC church roots because when I find myself between rocks and hard places, my heart inevitably and immediately goes to the cross.

Rumor has it that preacher's kids are the worst, and while I won't say explicitly that I agree, I will say that I am so far from perfect that it isn't even funny. While much of this collection is focused on God, there are also pieces and stories that relate to some mistakes I've made, some mistakes I've thought about making, and the lessons I've learned from both.

What I hope you receive from the reading of this collection is that no matter who you are, what you've done, or what you may plan to do… God will love you in the midst of your mess. Believe me, because I know from experience.

Whether you go to church, or not… whether you believe in the bible, or not… whether you *care,* or not… the love that He/ She has for you is undeniable.

Some of you may have read that and concluded that I am crazy because your current situation doesn't give you the capital to believe what I just said, and that's ok. I hope that by the time you reach the back cover of this book, you are encouraged to believe in yourself, your purpose, and God's plan for your life.

I began to use writing as an outlet as a sophomore in college and I found inspiration and admiration in writers like Zora Neale Hurston, Maya Angelou, Nikki Giovanni and Rupi Kaur.

Nikki Giovanni's extended use of metaphors has always intrigued me, and this collection reflects that inspiration. From Maya Angelou, I learned the impact of creating stories that told themselves. From Zora Neale Hurston, I learned the value of being unapologetic about the things I create and Rupi Kaur taught me how to get my point across with only the words that matter… not the ones that don't.

This collection is dedicated to Alma Lee Smith, because everything I do, I do for her.

A Stranger

I don't know who you are, but you feel like a gentle kiss upon a cheek.

I don't know who you are, but you look so much like me.

I don't know who you are, and I certainly wish I did.

I don't know who you are, but there was death so you could live.

...Who Passed Through

this wasn't the first time our souls crossed paths.
and it certainly won't be the last.
do not cry for me. Don't you dare weep...
because we will find each other once again.

For You...

I wish Heaven Had a Phone

If heaven had a phone
I swear I'd call you every day.
I'd be getting on God's nerve,
Tryna evaluate your stay.

If visiting hours were a thing,
I'd see you every week
And I'd bring pictures every time,
So you could see what came of me.

If I could see your face each day,
Or simply hear your voice…
I'd walk through life with happiness,
And my heart'd be filled with joy.

I love you more than you'd ever know,
And perhaps that's hard to say.
Because after I think about it,
You've looked out for me every single day.

Although I cannot see you…
And I cannot head you speak,
I know that you are with me,
Lending peace when I am weak.

I know you got hella pull!
Cause you and God are mad tight!

And I know you'd go to war with Him,
If it meant I'd be alright.
People think I'm crazy…
Because sometimes I talk to trees.
And that's too bad for them,
Because the trees wave back at me.

Everything I do,
I do to make you proud.
Because you had such high hopes for me,
And I'd hate to let you down.

I wish heaven had a phone.
So I could call you every day…
So I could get on God's nerve,
Just to insure that you're ok.

For Alma

I don't Think Angels Know Who They Are

Have you ever met someone whose heart was well
seasoned?
I mean… someone whose love *really* tastes good?
The whole hood rocks with them and they rock
back with the hood?

Have you ever met someone whose kindness
almost scared you?
I mean… someone whose *way* too kind?
Someone who speaks for those without, and is
generous with their time?

I hope one day you meet someone
Any you know the second that you greet,
They were sent to be your guardian,
To protect you when you sleep.

I pray one day you cross paths with someone
From a different city and a different street.
And time breathes a little deeper in that moment,
so at your journey, you can peak.

For Ms. Leighton

Queendom Kid

I know that God is real because she's my mother.
She is my Shepard, I shall not want.
 I believe in her existence because I don't know
anyone else who could do what she does.
Oceans cease at her command; Mountains shift.
The Earth quakes when she stretches her hands
And Tsunamis are caused by one switch in her hip.

I know God is real because she's my best friend.
She maketh me to lie down in green pastures –
she leads me beside still waters - she restores my
soul.
I couldn't hide anything from her if I wanted to.

She knows every mistake-
She knows every malicious thought-
She knows every insecurity-
She knows.

I know God is real because she's my daughter.
Yea though I walk through the valley of the
shadow of death, I will fear no evil for she is with
me.
When she smiles, my heart beams.
Her existence alone is a reality check for my
selfishness-
and her happiness is enough to make or break me.

I know God is real because she lives in me.
*She prepares a table before me in the presence of
mine enemies: she anoints my head with oil. My
cup…*
My cup… My cup runneth over.

When I breathe, she breathes too.
When I walk, she walks too.
When I weep, she weeps too.
When I smile, she smiles too.

*And surely …. Surely goodness and mercy shall
follow me all the days of my life; and I will dwell
in the house of the Lord forever.*

Amen.

    For my unborn daughter

Black Boys in Bomber Jackets

You can't wear that bomber jacket.

For those Jordan's I can't provide payment.
Cause if the wrong white person sees you,
Your face could be smashed on the pavement.

Not for any wrong doing,
not for passing through the wrong hood…
but simply for being a black boy,
whose childhood is often misunderstood.

I can't let you learn to drive.
And I can't buy you a car.
Cause what if you get pulled over?
And for breathing, end up behind bars?

No you cannot go skating,
or to your high school prom…
Cause your life is far too valuable,
for me to no longer be your mom.

I can't let you leave my sight.
No matter how old you get.
Cause all it takes is one wrong move,
and my boy'd be put to rest.

If peace could pass all time and space
And love could heal all wounds…
Then you could wear that bomber jacket,
And I would buy you them new shoes.

  For my unborn son

Count it all Physical

If you counted each obstacle as a physical attack, could you dust yourself off and stand?

If everything that went wrong in life, you could equate to a punch or blow, could you dust yourself off and stand?

If the only things in life that hit you, were sticks and stones alone… could you dust yourself off and stand?

And if you get knocked down by man, could you dust yourself off and stand?

Universal Virtue

If patience could hold you where you are,
then space and time my heart'd defy.
And lust could harmonize to curse the tears we cry.

If everyone could work in peace, and we all just do
our parts,
Belief could grant us hope and truth.
If patience could hold you where you are…

A wish that we could bind like ocean and bay,
Or a love unknown to you and I
And lust could harmonize to curse the tears we cry.

This pain we share, outsiders stare
And life may have you strung at the neck, but
If patience could hold you where you are…

A conceptualization of God's purpose says
It takes six plus one to = your dream
And lust could harmonize to curse the tears we cry.

From the abundance of the heart, may our mouths speak.
Hear, remind, and convince yourself
If patience could hold you where you are,
That string of life around your neck will burn as strange fruit. [1]

---

[1] Billie Holiday alludes to the lynching of Black people in the song "Strange Fruit", 1954.

Sis

She steps first with her left, only to be followed by her right,
she answers questions either directly or not at all
because with her there is only black or white.

She burns sage as she wakes to protect and harness her light,
acknowledging and respecting her ancestral plight.

She sings in the morning and she hums at night,
constantly in thought about the wars she must fight.

She dances in the evening, clenching tight to her dreams,
of bringing joy to the world by raising children of a king.

She cries in the morning, just before she heads to work,
but she manages to stand cause her bag always comes first!

She hates the concept of carpools, cause when she's ready she must go!
and if you ever ride with her, she'll leave yo ass fo sho!

She may not ever fully love you, cause her heart is still too sick,
and she'll never claim you publicly, cause to her you're just dick.

Inevitable

You went yesterday.
I'm came today.
…and we both arrived.

You ate fast,
I ate slow...
…and we both are fed.

You cried for her.
I cried for him.
…and we both wept.

Untitled

I met this woman today.
who was mad as hell and probably didn't even
know why.

she had hate in her heart and tears rising in her
eyes
she walked side by side with aggression and her
goals were very clear

to tear down everything around her
and set fire to all that came near.

she told jokes to the devil,
for which he'd often chuckle hard.

and she gossiped with her demons
when friends weren't near or far.

A Sister's Prayer

May you never walk this earth alone,
For you now have sisters everywhere.

May you always have a helping hand,
With fellowship, and laughter, and care.

May your every step be ordered,
Because those before you have paved the way.

And may you know, at every bend in the road,
The right things to do, to think, and to say.

Welcome to this sisterhood, we're so glad you
came.
As of today, your life will never be same.

For Spring '19

Untitled

We don't wanna "touch our neighbors" or "tell our neighbors a DAMN thing! We came for the word! DASSIT!

For the bored minister

No Words

Too Hot to spark, too cold to freeze.
Too wet to drip, too tired to sleep.

Too heavy to anchor, to light to float.
To tight to fit, too rigid to coat.

Too passionate to resist, too painful to feel.
Too broken to fix, too damaged to heal.

Too happy to laugh, too excited to smile.
Too engaged to depart, too sad to cry.

Too lucky to chance, too trapped to stay put.
Too confused to clarify, too strong to push.

Too patient to wait, too stuck to sit still.
Too honest to tell the truth, too deadly to kill.

Too drunk to stagger, too high to float.
Too ready for round 2, too friendly for folk.

Too Christian to worship, too holy for church.
Too selfish to say no, too giving to serve.

Too strong to hold on, too weak to let go.
Too depressed to sleep in, too fluid to flow.

Too fast to crash, too slow to roll.
Too magical to conjure, too hopeless to fold.

Pressure on the Crown

I know yo' head is heavy.
cause u can't get nowhere and sit down.
you keep adding shit to ya' plate,
and putting pressure on yo' crown.

I know you're tired
cause u won't stop and just sit still.
you think you'll miss your chance,
so you keep your days and weeks filled.

I know you've lost yourself
in the midst of all these tasks
you probably ain't take ya' vitamins today
I'm not even gonna ask.

I know your eyes are low
cause you smoked to get out of bed.
and you probably took a shot too;
you claim it clears ya' head.

I know ya' body aches
and you haven't slept all week.
cause u stretched ya' self too thin,
and you can't slow ya' feet!

I know yo' head is heavy.
cause u can't get nowhere and sit down.

you keep adding shit to ya' plate,
and putting pressure on yo' crown.

Dream Chasing

I used to think that chasing dreams was only for
the privileged . for those with spoons of silver and
lives unchallenged.

I thought success was only offered to the elite
and the only seats at the table were for those who
could eat.

I imagined prosperity, but not for myself cause I
didn't have support, or generational wealth.

I thought I had to afford my dreams but I learned
my dreams afforded me.

I used to think that chasing dreams was only for
the privileged . for those with spoons of silver and
lives unchallenged.

Untitled

ashes to ashes
dust to dust
you had me twisted and
you got me fucked up...

Indecisive

I want you... but only sometimes...

I kind of wanna love you, but my heart just won't
give in.
Love can be blinding; and I refuse to mirror kin.

It's not without difficulty though, because I do
wish that I could.

I wish that I could see past my damage but... I'm
good.

Foundation

You have splits running up your walls that you keep trying to paint over.

Your floors are pulling themselves up by the bootstraps and your ceiling is cracked.

Have you checked your foundation?

Your windows won't close all the way. The pipes squeak when you turn on the faucets.

The kitchen tiles are falling apart and it's the same in the bathroom.

Have you checked the foundation?

the sidewalk is splitting in two. your porch is leaning, and the steps aren't sturdy.

Have you checked the foundation?

Forbidden fruit

I could rip you from your skin a million times over
I could grant you peace within and when all is said
and done I can hold your head upon my chest and
tell you that I love you. I hate that you don't k ow
who you are but I honestly wouldn't have it any
other way.

On this realm we are friends. We met through what
we both call chance and God but here we are just
friends. On other realms, however, our relationship
is different. In realms above us we are lovers and
soulmates. On realms below us we are enemies
and foes. I pray I never slip below, because I'd
never want to fight you. But I hope each night, as I
fall into R.E.M. that I can find you up above.
Because up above you make me feel unwanted by
the world but your heart's sole desire. It's like the
things that matter to you here, don't matter to you
there.

In past lives we were one soul, which time and
death hath split. so when I met you I knew that you
were me... or maybe I was you. I don't know but it
really doesn't matter... because while we're
dreaming... I just want you to just undress before
we wake.

Sometimes I wonder who we were before this life... and I think about all the possibilities. But in all honesty I don't think I could bare the knowing. If I knew exactly who you were, I'd want to go to sleep forever, I'm sure. Because with you time stands still in ways we as humans will never comprehend. with you there is peace. With you my SOUL is alright.

Children could be born

With your girth and my grip, children could be born.

With your stroke and my choke, children could be born.

If you get lost and I forget, children could be born.

Skeletons

Could you take it to the grave?

Could you live your entire life knowing what lives inside your closet?

Could you lie to yourself forever?

Could you…?

Time

Yesterday you were my friend.

Today you are my lover.

Tomorrow I may let you love me back.

Triggered...

I need for you to stop, but I can't quite tell u what.

It's like whatever you are doing is making me cringe.

I don't want it.

why can't you read my mind? or at least my body language?

I need for you to stop.

I don't want the love you give. At least not today.

My Bad

I'm sorry…

And although I shouldn't be,

I find myself in frequent regret

I apologize… and even though it's not my fault,

I feel as though it should be.

Where are you?

Where is love? when you need it but don't want it?

Where is God? When you've fallen but don't have strength to stand?

Where is peace? When you've lost your mind but don't care to look for it?

A Letter from a Coward

Sometimes I avoid your eyes because you can see straight through me.

I can't look at you,

My eyes tell truths I don't want you to know.

I can't be around you,

My spirit reveals secrets my heart won't tell.

I can't talk to you…

Because the space between my words won't hide the untold.

I want to.. really I do, but I'm unable.

For Me…

Excuses...

She is 100% incompetent.

She makes excuses in an effort to build bridges
that lead in the opposite direction of you.

She uses them to build monuments in her head that
make you amount to nothingness.

Because she uses excuses... she may never find
specialty in your love.

I found myself today

I was walking past a coffee shop and I saw me. I sat in a window with a book in one hand and a mug in the other.

I had long kinky hair, paper sack colored skin, and even though I had never seen myself before, I knew I could trust me.

I looked up at me, while I stood in my gaze and I tipped the nose of my glasses, and noticed... we were jus the same.

Not a word needed to be said, I knew who I was. I simply patted the table and said "I'm so glad that you came".

"You've done good this far, really you have, but if you don't mind, I'll carry us the rest of the way."

"You see, there are things we need that only I can attain and there are obstacles we must conquer for which you aren't yet trained."

"You'll have to let me lead, cause where we are going, only I know the way. And you'll have to stay close, bad things may happen if you stray."

"We're going on a journey and listen close for only once I will mention. I'm taking you to where I live but you'll have to pay close attention."

"I'll give you all the keys, but it's your job to unlock the doors and I'll go before you every day, to turn your ceilings into floors."

"What's all that, in the bags you carry?" I asked asked... "oh no sweetheart you can't bring these they're far too heavy".

"See where we're going, we must travel by foot, and if all these things you insist on keeping, you may as well stay put."

"I'll take out this sadness, cause it'll only slow us down. And I'll remove this depression cause I don't wanna see you frown"

"I'll toss out this old bag of insecurities, you got stuff in here from birth! And you don't need this anxiety anymore, that's the wearing of earth"

"Why do you still have this trauma, it's not even yours! It was passed down to you like used clothes and hand-me-down toys".

"Ima gone head and get rid of this stress cause it's just a thorn in your side, and ima trash this procrastination cause from now on you gone do shit on TIME!"

"I'll take away this hurt, cause with me you'll hurt no more. And I'll replace it with love you can carry at your core"

"I'll wash your muddy heart and repair it's cracks and pieces. And I'll trash all this resentment you tried to hide inside the creases".

"Now that all that's gone, let's look at what is left. Let's see if what u have is a reflection of myself".

"I'll take all your dreams, and your biggest aspirations. I'll I'll turn them into truths, in exchange for a little patience".

"Look at all these good things you hid at the bottom of your bag! It's a shame you stifled their growth, it's really kinda sad".

"You hid your creativity and it got smushed by all your crap! Didn't anybody ever teach you to always pack the bread last?"

"I cannot show you everything, cause it's too much to understand. And on the days you cannot trace my hand, just trust I know my plan".

"It may get cloudy down the road. you may claim that you can't see, but know that I am with you, placing pavement to your feet".

"You may get tired along the way and that's perfectly ok. You can rest if you must, but from my watch you'll never stray".

"But this one thing I ask of you. If you rest, don't rest too long. You'll have a lot of catching up to do because I'm going to keep moving on".

"It won't be hard to find me, because my footsteps I'll leave for you to follow. And if you can't find me on today, I'll come find you on tomorrow".

I met myself today and she told me all these things, about the places I'll go and the things I cannot bring.

The Appointment

You kissed me gently once or twice
then told me to undress,
and upon our drunken understanding,
we met with patience and finesse.

This act of lust…I must explain
will end in consequence
and although we both were made aware,
we fought both self-control and wit.

You need me and I need you,
but only in that space.
cause what you thought would end in love
may double as disgrace.

you are but a floating dream
a vibey track played on repeat.
a gentle melody,
That skipped my heart it's beat.

move your hand and let me in,
I want to give you peace.
these few things passed through my ears
and shivers through your feet.

You kissed me gently once or twice
then laid upon my chest,

and when you fell asleep that night,
I grabbed my shit and left.

Mirror Work

Have you seen me lately?
I haven't seen her in a while and I don't know
where she went.

You aren't me… I don't recognize you. WHERE
AM i? WHERE DID SHE GO?

Why did I leave? And when can I expect her to
return?

If you won't tell me where I've gone, just reassure
me that she's ok and she will come back soon.

This Ain't Brewster Street[2]

You gone have to move and make room for some peace.

Because this ain't 1989 and you don't live on Brewster street.

Your sun may not shine each day and you may not find shade from trees.

But thank God this ain't 1989 and you don't live on Brewster street.

You have far too many bills, and not enough to make ends
meet.

But just be grateful that this ain't 1989 and you don't live on Brewster street.

[2] Brewster Street is a fictional setting from the book, turned motion picture miniseries, "Women of Brewster Place" (1989, Harpo's Productions) where black women were separated from the rest of the world through a physical brick wall symbolizing racism, poverty, violence and sexism.

Talk to me Nice

Run me a bath, put Epsom salt in the tub, pour me a glass of $5 Aldi wine, light a candle and talk to me nice.

Sit on the edge of the tub, feed me red seedless grapes, tell me about your day and talk to me nice.

Wrap me in a bath sheet from a luxury target line, rub baby oil on my skin, tell me how much you love me and talk to me nice.

Lay me on a fresh set of sheets, rub my back, rub my feet, massage my booty and talk to me nice.

Rest my head on your chest, rub coconut oil on my scalp, hug me tight and talk to me nice.

Make me a turkey sandwich with tomatoes, lettuce, onion and cheese. Slice it down the middle, bring it to me on a plastic plate with some purple Kool-Aid and talk to me nice.

Take out my trash, fill up my car with premium gas, carry my luggage inside the airport for me and talk to me nice.

Make me a playlist. Fill it with songs that remind you of me. Send me one track a week and talk to me nice.

Ask me to cook you some pasta, then eat my food like it's running away from you and talk to me nice.

Text me on Sunday mornings and ask me if I'm getting ready for church. Tell me you can't wait to see me and talk to me nice.

Hug me tight when it's cold, stay away from me when it's hot and talk to me nice.

Buy me expensive shit, no matter how much I tell you not to and talk to me nice.

Send me nudes on your afternoon lunch break, (put a lil oil on first) and talk to me nice.

Take me to the edge of my favorite body of water, hold my hand and ask me about my fears. Talk to me nice.

Rain

We exchange correspondence in the rain.

I speak untold secrets in the rain.

Patience, purpose and vision are gifts brought by the rain.

I talk to God and she responds in the rain.

Darkness isn't so dark in the rain.

Tears of sadness and joy dance together in the puddles left behind,

And just like every good thing, the rain will end.

Friend and Associate

My anxiety likes to visit, *just* when I do not need her. She comes so often I even made up the guest room. Sometimes she'll sleep there. Sometimes she'll insist on sleeping with me. Sometimes, she'll stay on her side of the bed. Other times, she'll snuggle right up under me. Sometimes she won't hogg the blanket, and other times she will. Sometimes she won't snore, but often times, she will.

My anxiety visits me so much, I decided to give her a name. because I've adopted her as a part of me, I figured we could share names. Why not? We share everything else. We share food because when she wants what I've eaten, I'm forced to throw it up. Every person we've been with has had to experience us both. If I make love, she has sex. If I find intimacy, she finds conversation.

We can't ever be on the same page. We share goals but not the execution of those goals because she refuses to help me accomplish them. She won't accept change because she likes what we have right now. She likes where we are in life right now and she doesn't want to move.

Eventually, she moved in full time. She became my most craved comfort at night. She became my deepest desire and my most precious day dream.

I used to text her in the middle of my work day, just to see how she was doing. I drove 13 minutes home each day at lunch to see her and hug her. We would eat lunch together for 30 minutes, and then I'd drive those 13 minutes back to the office and finish my day.

She and I are bound by insecurity. I'm afraid that if I dismiss her from my life, I'll never find another friend to love me the way she does. One thing's for sure, she DEFINITELY loves me. She has always shown up when no other friend has. She's the friend I don't have to work for. She's the one I don't have to beg for. She just shows up.

Peace on the other hand, she's more like an associate. She comes around every now and then but only after I've prayed and cried and begged God to let her come visit. *Peace* requires much more effort. Peace won't come to my house if it isn't clean. She won't come near me until I've forgiven the people in my life who hurt me. She won't show up unless I meet her requirements.

Peace forces me to get out of bed when I don't want to. She forces me to be honest with myself and those around me. *Peace* forces me to seek the assistance of mental health professionals. *Peace* won't let me do what I want to do.

Peace is a much nicer house guest than *anxiety*. When peace visits, she cooks full meals, she pays bills, she returns phone calls and she doesn't hog the blanket. In fact, when peace visits, she brings extra covering and we rest well together without stirring.

However, despite how amazing peace is, I don't see her as often because she's a little more strict than anxiety. Peace comes with structure and responsibilities. Anxiety doesn't care if I don't clean my dishes for a week, but peace will shake me from my sleep and say "girl get yo ass up and wash them dishes". Or… "when I went to bed last night, didn't I tell you to take out the trash?"

Anxiety will encourage my compulsive sexual encounters, peace won't let me lay under someone I don't love.

Anxiety will roll me a blunt, pour me a glass of wine and convince me I'm deserving of relaxation.

Peace will take me to the gym and run with me until my heart creeps on explosion.

Anxiety will take me to the river and ask me to jump in but Peace… *will bring the river to me*.

Consequences

Fat meat must not be greasy,
cause you act like you don't know.
that your actions come with results,
and consequences come with blows.

You must think you can run away...
from all the problems you create
and that the words you chose to use,
somehow have no weight.

You have got to be crazy,
if you think these beds made themselves.
And you must be a fool,
to think you could do it all yourself.

Mother

I am not my mother.
She is not me.
We are not each other,
and ourselves we will never be.

A Letter to my heart

I can't feel you anymore. Are you still there?
Did you move from left to right?
Did you disappear?
Will you return tonight?

I can't hear you beating. Did you die?
Did you fade away like dust?
Did you crawl up in a ball and cry?
Will you come back at dusk?

I can't see you anymore. You used to smile
through faces of strangers.
Did you stop smiling?
Will you ever smile again?

I Can't Fail

I don't wanna fail cause although there are lessons to be learned, I'd rather get soaring right the first time than land face first in the dirt.

tell me all your initial mistakes first and I'll figure out how not to fail. just give me the blueprint you used and I'll examine the breadcrumbs of your left behind trail.

I'll have to account for secondary variables like location, network, and time, but if I play these cards right and do what I'm told, I'll be successful... right?

I don't wanna fail. I got too much on the line. I have so many things to accomplish and not quite enough time.

I gotta get it right from *jump*! Cause I don't have room for 2nd tries. I have to kick this list before I finally close my eyes.

I AM MUSIC

I am the millimeter of space that separates the fingertips of Nat King Cole from the white alabaster keys of his famous grand piano.

I am the interval that proceeds Nina Simone's 1st key change in 'feeling good'.

I am the last slant rhyme in Cole's explicit version of 'no role models' from forest hills.

I... Am... Music

I am the woven fabric that shields the breast of Erykah Badu,

I am the last HOOK of the last TRACK of your most admired artists first mixtape.

I am the scribbles on the pages of a black and white composition notebook of a dreamer who once dreamed a dream the jealous world later took!

I... Am... Music

I am the melody of the chorus that is "the way" by Jill Scott.

I am the broken sentences of the two line couplet of the poem that reached consciousness but never met thought.

I am the soul in the voice of the eldest mother of your oldest black Penni costal or COGIC church.

I... Am... Music

I am the unspoken harmony that exists inside the heart ties of a woman and her child. The ties that make possible an awareness of a 500 mile cry.

I am the rosin that coats the bows of the violins of a symphonic orchestra.

I am the smooth that gyrates from the vocal chords of Lauren Hill, the smooth that later falls delicately from her lips and spill.

I... Am... Music

I am the wave that is the vibrato of a Musik Souldchild track.

I am the resonance of the greatest song of the greatest album, of the greatest artist that every lived.

I am the unshakable tune of the jingle of your most viewed network television commercial.

I… Am… Music

I am the coldest lyric of the dopest verse of the sharpest tune you'll ever hear.

I am the soliloquy that drowns the background beat and the underlying instrumental.

I am the traction from your fingertips when you finally introduce paper to pencil.

Dear Mamma,

I'm sorry that I hated you and I hate that I had to.

I wish that I could erase my words, or that they didn't have truth.

I don't wish that I could see you, but I do hope that you are well.

And if you were here, to your face I would tell.

I had so many questions, about when your life turned for the bad.

Why did you stay so long? You must've been very sad.

If I were you, I would've left much sooner, cause life was cruel to you.

But in life's defense, you made your beds. They didn't make you.

For God…

Sunday Mornin'

Do what you want on Saturday night,

But have yo ass in a pew Sunday mornin'.

Don't care how much you had to drink, or how much tree you got in ya lungs,

Just have you ass in a pew Sunday mornin'.

Don't matter who you rolled off of at 10am,

Just betta have that ass in church pew Sunday mornin'.

I don't care how many errands you need to run… shoulda did that shit yesterday,

You betta have you ass in a church pew on Sunday morning.

Haven't had breakfast? Still in ya Fenty® from last night? That's alright…

Just have yo ass in a church pew on Sunday morning.

Give her you

For every obstacle in her way, give her fortitude.
For every mountain she must climb, give her strength.
For every battle she must fight, give her armor.
For every tear she must cry, give her comfort.
For everything she must lose, give her more.
For every storm she must weather, give her shelter.
For every 'no' she must hear, tell her 'yes'.
For every lonely night, give her peace.
For every broken heart, give her pacification.
For every obstruction she must face, give her structure.
For every interruption, give her motivation.
For every handicap she may encounter, grant her endurance.
For every bridge she must cross, grant her access.
For every table in which she has interest, bring her a seat.
For every goal her mind creates, clear her vision.
For every sickness she'll encounter, grant her healing.

And for every question she may have, give her *you*.

But they see God

The woman in your mirror sees failure,
But the homeless man she shares change with sees
God.

The woman who wears your socks and combs your
hair agonizes over flaws,
But the lady she passes in the elevator on the way
to work sees God.

The woman that sits in your skin feels cold and
alone,
But the children she birthed and nursed see God.

These feet that carry her are bruised and they hurt,
But the people who she shares this journey with
see God.

The glue that holds her family together is on the
verge or wearing thin,
But her siblings and her parents see God.

The wall she built around her heart has just been
improved,
But the man whose in love with her sees God.

For Her Leaves

I asked a tree for her leaves
and she gave me foes.

I asked her for her branches
and she gave me friends.

I asked her for her trunk
and she gave me shelter.

I asked her for her roots
and she gave me you.

Questions

How do you breathe…
when the air has been taken from you?

How do you walk…
when your legs have been cut from underneath
you?

How do you talk… when your tongue has been
carved?

How do you eat… when food no longer has
flavor?

How do you speak… when your mouth can't form
words?

How do you love... when your heart no longer
works properly?

How do you breathe?

The Water

TAKE ME TO THE WATER[3]

I wonder what would happen... if I fell into the water.

would I sink or would I swim? if I fell into the water.

I wonder how I'd breathe if I fell into the water.

or if for my life, I'd plead, if I fell into the water

TAKE ME TO THE WATER

I wonder if I'd float... if I fell into the water

or if that'd be all she wrote... if I fell into the water.

I wonder what they'd think of I fell into the water think

TAKE ME TO THE WATER

or if at my wake, you'd drink if I fell into the water.

---

[3] "Take Me To The Water" is a common hymn sung during African American baptism ceremonies.

would I rise from this bad dream if I fell into the water?

or would my sins be washed clean if I fell into the water.

TO BE BAPTIZED
Welcome to forever,

a place you thought you'd never find.

A place that can only be reached...

through transformation of the mind.

Welcome to eternity, a world inside it's world.

You thought you'd never make it, but it's finally your turn.

Welcome to forever. We hope you find it in your heart to stay.

But Forever can't be forever, if all nights must end by day.

Bigger than us

I believe that God is female
and her smile stretches wide like rolling seas.
I believe that she is beautiful and that she looks
just like me.

I bet you God is soft,
like the skin around our knees when we fall on
them talk, give thanks or plead.

god must be a goddess…
cause her tone is far too sweet,
and I hope that she embraces me the second that
we meet.

she told me she's a woman,
when I wouldn't listen to a man.
and she grabbed me by my ear and forced me to
stand.

she must be a woman,
with an abundance of love.
who touched me like no man ever could.

her love for us is perfect,
and unlike her son, we bleed in vain…

cause what we fail to realize is that this is all just a crazy game.

Psalm 23

Yea Though I walk…

Nobody in this room looks like me. I don't know shit about "The Office" of "Game of Thrones". I cant relate to anything these people are talking about.

Through the Valley of the shadow of death…

I wonder if they think I'm here because I'm lucky. I wonder if they think I deserve to be here as much as they do.

I will fear no evil

Actually… I'm lowkey smarter than some of them. I think critically to find imaginative solutions and I never half ass anything! If ima do it, it's gone be done RIGHT.

For thou art with me…

I do deserve to be here. I do deserve every opportunity I have.

Thy Rod and Thy Staff, they comfort me.

Don't you Know Who I am?

Why Must you worry? Why must you stress?
Did you not believe me when I said you'd have the
best?

Why won't you trust me? Why must you fight so
hard?
You're tripping over battles when I've already
won the war.

You're trying to dig up mountains when I only
asked you to climb;
And you keep avoiding my instruction… wasting
energy and time.

Be still My child. Don't you know who I am?
I am God by myself, and I always have a plan.

Mamma Said

MAMMA SAID GO WASH THEM DISHES

She thought the suds would run away if I didn't. She said I'd regret it if I didn't.

MAMMA SAID YOU CAN'T GO WITHOUT ME

She was sure I wouldn't return if I did. She knew I'd leave with no regret if I did.

MAMMA SAID I COULDN'T DO IT

So I asked God instead.

An Ego Trip[4]

"I'm so hip, even my errors are correct".

When I dance, the heels of my shoes don't even touch the ground.

When I laugh, my soul spills into the eyes of children.

For a Kwanzaa gift, I gave my son Saturn and he cried because what he really wanted was the Moon.

Patience is my middle name because time waits at my feet.

I don't open doors, they are opened for me. They remain open for my friends and closed to my enemies.

I become oceans when I cry, and deserts when I dry my tears.

I am the lava the spills from eruptions of Kamakou and the ashes I leave behind become grounding for you to stand.

"I'm so hip, even my errors are correct".

---

[4] This piece is a play on my favorite piece ever written. Nikki Giovanni's poem "Ego Trippin" is an anthem, written with the intention to invoke pride among black women.

I have Vibranium in my veins and my ligaments are made from elastic gold.

If you cut me, I'd bleed honey and if you hit me, I won't bruise.

Proverbs Three and Sixteen

I am Wisdom and I am woman.

Find Me.

I hold prosperity in my right hand and success in my left.

Find Me.

I am sweeter than the nectar of flowers

Find Me.

My offspring are humble.

Find Me.

… And when you find me, trust me.

A Stranger

I don't know who you are, but you feel like a gentle kiss upon a cheek.

I don't know who you are, but you look so much like me.

I don't know who you are, and I certainly wish I did.

I don't know who you are, but there was death so you could live.

...Who Passed Through

this wasn't the first time our souls crossed paths.
and it certainly won't be the last.
do not cry for me. Don't you dare weep...
because we will find each other once again.

MAPACHA

A Short Story

For the mother,
Who is also the sister…
And the daughter too.

Friday, 4:00pm

I closed my notebook, placed all my writing utensils into a decretive cup I was gifted for managing, somehow, to become the first college graduate in my immediate family, wiped off my desk and keyboard with a Clorox wipe and loaded up my small white office box with only gadgets I had accumulated over the past 6 months. A utensil holder, a premium stapler I received at an office Christmas party a few months ago, 6 bandaids, 2 college rulled notebooks with scribblings from a project that spent 4 months to bring to fruition and a framed piece of art from a coworker who likes to draw.

I drive a Mini Van

There are quite frequent occasions in which I am tasked with the responsibility of caring for my 6-year-old niece. **Thank you mommy,** Jada said to me from the back seat of my minivan as I was transporting her to Head Start one morning. I had purchased a small red bear and gifted it to her inside a sparkling silver bag along with some white and faded red tissue paper from the Dollar Tree. A very special celebration would take place that afternoon at her school. After recess on this particular day, the head start directors would run 3 feet behind Jada and her classmates to enforce the significance of the bell that would ring each weekday promptly at 1:00. Upon entrance into the classroom, kids scream and yell in excitement as they each find a treat bag filled with snickers and twizzlers, and popcorn balls, and nerds, and anything else they could've dreamed of, nicely arranged on their respective circles of the story mat. Jada would walk to her desk and find a treat bag that was much more elaborate than that of her fellow classmates and it came with a note that Jada would have to ask her head start director to translate. *I love you, Mommy.*

Cold Hands

Rho has a really annoying habit of putting her hands inside of my shirt and pressing her palms against my upper back. As children, skin to skin contact would comfort each of us equally but as we have aged, grown, developed, changed… I am less appreciative, and she is more desperate for comfort of the sort. *Oooo I'm sorry* my sister whispered, *Damn Rho! Get back!*
Friday, 5:00pm

As I pull into the two-car garage my sister and I share, a red gas tank symbol appears on the dashboard of my 2015 Dodge Caravan and is complemented with a *ding.* Before I can even open my car door, I am greeted with a warm smile, a bouncy body and angelic laughter. ***Jada step back so you don't get hit with this car door!*** I shout behind the air tight window. ***Hi mommy!*** She shouts back. ***Jada… remember your mom has short hair?*** I briskly correct her while stealthily checking for any sign her mother may be within ear's distance.

Today is the kind of day that sits on your chest; the weight enough to constrict your lungs only until the *edge* of collapse.
Today is the kind of day that you sleep next to but don't recognize in the morning.
Today is like the moment you realize you are catching a cold.
Today is like the orange tint on your Tupperware.

Today… is *that* kind of day.

It's a Girl

With her feet secured in stirrups, and knees as close to the mattress as physically possible, my mother pushed, and pressed, and strained and screamed, and prayed and begged, and cried. ***It's a girl!***

With her arms gripping the railing of a hospital bed and forehead glistening with the sweat of strain, *our* mother wailed, and moaned, and sobbed, and pouted, and cursed and wept. ***It's another girl…***

Friday, 9:00pm

Delightful, is the most suiting word to describe the meal my sister prepared. We gathered around a *lovely* extra-large, tightly packed, carefully sealed, cardboard wardrobe box. Our one course meal was *tastefully* organized in a Styrofoam cup. The ratio of noodle to juice was *exceptional* and the rehydrated vegetables were quite honestly, the star of the dish. To top it all off, she added a *refreshing,* chill and sugary brown beverage from a clear drink pitcher with a royal blue lid and mustard colored collapsible spout to complement the meal.

The picture frame left a mark

Staring at the barren walls of the estate I would soon cease to call home, an impeccable and flawless rectangle of dust stared me in the eye. It's 90 degree corners were sharp… and spiny… and pointy. The lines running parallel to the floor and ceiling pointed in each direction of the hallway that connected an adolescent pair. At one end was a room that used to contain my bed, dresser, night stand, tv. The other end of the hall exists a room that at one point in time housed my sister's bed, her dresser, her night stand, her tv.

On this wall, within the four corners of this dusty rectangle, used to reside a family portrait that gave my father… *our* father more credit than he deserved. The portrait portrays him as a great parent and spouse with my sister and I positioned on his lap and our mother standing just off his right shoulder. Her left hand lay delicately on the shoulder of my father and you would meet each face in the photo with a smile. The Christmas card of a portrait had a note on the back of it's frame. ***Mwili and Roho at 2 years.***

What my mother could not give

Does is taste nasty? Rho looks up with unconvincing eyes. ***No baby girl, it's clean… I promise.*** Rho proceeded to touch him. He pays no attention to her eyes and is much more interested in what she starts to do with her mouth. He thinks her mouth feels like home. Her mouth makes him feel like a *man*. Because of her mouth, he can conquer his world and because of her mouth he will forever live in hers. It is in her mouth that he will find his purpose, his peace, his ability to live rather than simply exist.

The discussion

We hardly ever spoke, we didn't have to. I already knew what she would say and she knew what I'd say too.
In elementary school we learned, in a drastically traumatic accident, that if one twin gets hurt, the other one bears the bruise.

In middle school, she bore my insecurities and I bore hers…

Oh! And by the time we got to high school, we were *basically* the same person.

Friday, 10:00pm

We cleared the table that we made from the side of a wardrobe box, bagged away our Styrofoam cups and plastic forks, and breathed an equal sigh of completion. It was done. The house was all packed up, boxes aligned against a single wall in each room, the trash had been taken out and the only thing left out of place were the two Styrofoam cups and two plastic forks.

Last Will and Testament

...And to my sweet daughters, who have made my life worth living, I leave the house. I hope that it will bring you two closer. Now that I am gone, and you only have each other, heal... please.

Love Ma

Guardianship

Taking a series of pills or having a surgery could not save her. If she ended that life, she killed her sister and she killed her daughter.

A new home for Daddy

He eventually, after about 7 years or so, grew out of this *home* he had visited for so long. His attention shifted, he became distracted with work and life. Rho thought that giving him a new home would redirect his attention back to her. She prepared a more elaborate estate for her father. In this new home he would be made to feel like a king. In this new home, he ate three hot meals a day, all his work shirts were clean, and his car was always parked where he left it. This home that she made for him felt like a trip to the barbershop on the Saturday afternoon before Easter Sunday and this home gave him a line up that only God herself could improve. This home makes him forget. He forgets that the world is against him, and that his bills aren't paid and that he can't afford his mortgage and that his gas tank isn't empty. He forgets that he has entered the home of a woman who only exists because he entered the home of her mother some 17 years ago.

He comes in and examines the place, taking notes on how wonderful it is. ***Damn!*** He grabs a beer out of the fridge, sit's down on the couch, turns on the TV and thinks ***Fuck! I can't believe this is all mine.*** He adjusts the temperature, ***it's so warm*** and tries to mop the floor ***it's tooooo wet in here.***

Saturday, 5:00am

She's just as much mine as she is yours! I shout as I march past the stainless steal appliances, the sparkling marble countertops, and the hanging fern. *You didn't even want her* I scoff while moving through the arched door war, stepping down onto the cemented floor, walking to the left of the beams that separate my Caravan from her Camry, opening my car door and securing a peacefully snoring Jada into the backseat of my minivan. *I'll call the police!* She counters relentlessly but I respond, *and tell them what?*

She removes her hand from the garage door activation pad. Her body, a white flag, stands in the arched doorway. Behind her, a kitchen with stainless steel appliances and marble countertops and hanging ferns. In front of her, a rising darkness, a fleating memory. The garage door opens and a backdrop of the night sky rise into place seamlessly.

The keys jangle.
The engine starts.
The seatbelt clicks.
The tires move.

Daughter and Granddaughter

he'll have a few beers in the car,
he'll smoke a blunt when he gets to the door,
he'll take his rightful place on the couch, and when
he leaves,
he will leave something he had never left before.

Two hundred and seventy-one days later, a
chocolate skinned woman with silver hair in dark
blue scrubs will find me and our mother in the
waiting room of an inner-city hospital. ***It's a girl!***

The grandfather father had an extended-stay
vacation at a local penitentiary.

Saturday, 4:00pm

After what felt like an eternity on the road, I look up to see a peacefully resting Jada flooding the left half of my mirror and breathe as I pull into the garage of my apartment complex. ***It's so tall!*** She had never seen so many buildings so close together.

It's free

As long as there is breath in my body, all of her needs would be met and most of her desires fulfilled. She would have the coolest lunch box in elementary, she'd have the longest hair, and the prettiest face, and the best clothes out of her adolescent peers and she'd go to the best schools and have the best training and above all of those things I *can* buy, there's one thing she'll possess that I *can't*... kindness.

The End

www.ingramcontent.com/pod-product-compliance
Lightning Source LLC
Chambersburg PA
CBHW061152040426

42445CB00013B/1658